CW01522933

Peter Sloan Teaches
How to Troubleshoot P.C.'s
Become a P.C. Technician

by Peter Julius Sloan

Printed in June of 2011
Sloans Book Press
New York City, NY
10036

ISBN: 1-453-86846-1

Table of Contents

Introduction	3
1. Getting Certified	4
2. 32 Examples of House Calls	6
3. Hiring a Writer	40
4. Be your own writer. Use a template	41
5. Running a Classified Ad	44
6. Copyrighting Your Ad	45
7. Registering Your Business Name	47
8. Email Marketing Blast	51
9. Preserving Your Contacts	54
10. Accepting Payments Online/ by Phone	68
11. Start an E-Commerce Web Site	70
12. Have a Tax ID? Get a Business Phone & Email	73
13. Make a Local Flyer Campaign	74
14. More on Web Sites	76
15. Open a Business Banking Account	80
16. Don't Forget Self Employment Tax 27%	81
17. Congratulations, You Are Self Employed	82
18. A few tips on things to watch out for. Scam Alerts, Fraud	83

Introduction

While a senior at S.U.N.Y. I was working with a freelance web design client and stumbled across listing my services for web design and computer repair in the classifieds. I worked for over three years after graduation making over $300 every weekend as extra income aside from my job. I took post graduate computer science courses at New Horizons to get certified A+ Certified by CompTIA. After passing those courses along with a lot of extra hours working with Microsoft Office I was ready to get my business rolling as a full time freelance computer repair man. I got myself a tax ID from the IRS to be able to list my services as that of a company, got my merchant accounts working to accept credit card payments from my clients, ordered TurboTax Business Edition to keep track of my self employment tax, and ever since then am a vendor licensed to operate my own business in New York State. I learned how to request at 1099 from my clients for tax season and even opened business banking with Capital One. I am currently working on a broader advertising campaign allowing me to accept clients world wide who do not need in person services for selling web sites.

Working as a self employed IT is a sure fire way to always keep money in your pocket regardless of how the economy is going. Miss an appointment? Who cares. You are your own boss. There is no one upstairs to call you at 5pm and say "Sloan, You were late for your three o'clock, You're fired." A matter of fact if someone does try to spin into your classified ads and take your clients, they could be sued for infringement (See Chapter 5 'Copyrighting Your Ad').

Best wishes to you and your new business,

Peter Julius Sloan
A+, Net+, MCP
S.U.N.Y. Purchase Class of 2003, F.I.D.E. 2230
Department of Education Chess & Dell 2003 - 2008

Chapter 1: Getting Certified

There are many certifications that can make you a home P.C. Technician repair man. The CompTIA A+ Certification in one of them. Another one I picked up on the job was CISCO LinkSYS wireless tech. There are more certifications than that. Working for the cable company you can get an on the job Risc 3 certification for cable box repair. **HomePNA.org** offers certificates to become a home cable repair man perfect for freelance clients. CompTIA offers a Network+ exam on wired and wireless networks, Microsoft Offers exams in a variety of operating systems going all the way back to Windows NT. Dell offers at home online courses for teaching yourself how to diagnose computer problems, one of them called the Dell Diagnostic Engineer Training program, for $200 for one year.

For keeping track of your own clients I recommend taking classes in Microsoft Office Word Excel Outlook Access and also PowerPoint. I use excel and PayPal to invoice my clients, Outlook for keeping track of my client contacts, Word for writing new email scripts to prospective clients, and PowerPoint for making presentations and shows. Access is for the database end. You can achieve excellence in office with an Office Specialist certification from **Certiport.com** They offer certificates in Adobe Applications as well.

Goo web sites to visit
Microsoft.com/Learning
CompTIA.org
HomePNA.org
Certiport.com
Cisco.com

You will be directed to take a multiple choice certification exam. No one passes on the first try and it costs roughly $100 to take the exam each try. You have to go to a certified testing center, no different than taking a state license exam in Real Estate or Nursing. Unlike real estate licenses or series 7 for stocks the A+ Certification is valid for the lifetime of the recipient. I know marines who passed A+ 1997 (or earlier) to get promoted into the corporate world where they could work.

Take a look at my A+ Certificate here.

Good luck at the testing center.

Chapter 2: Examples of House Calls

We will now go over a 32 examples of house calls. In all of these examples your are the P.C. Technician making a house call based on an inquiry to your classified ad. The pay rate I follow is $60 per house call for up to three hours. $20 per hour there after. Remember it is a long standing tradition to offer IT services outside of the major companies such as J&R Computers and Time Warner Cable. A matter of fact, those companies prefer we operate our businesses because there are only so many calls Time Warner can take and only in regards to their own cable router. Any other call to fix a computer running Windows or Mac goes straight to the doorstep of our home business.

Example 1: You arrive at the site of your client who called complaining about trouble with there PC sound card.

There are a few steps involved to diagnose the problem.

1. Make sure the speakers are plugged in. This is the most common reason that a client cannot hear sound on there computer. Do not forget to make sure that the volume is turned up as well.
2. Check the mute button by using the speaker icon. Both windows XP and Vista have an icon for the speaker on the toolbar on the very lower right corner of the display. Double click on the icon and uncheck the mute button.
3. Drivers – Speaker drivers are very generic and do not require a hardware specific driver. By clicking on the Control Panel and going to add new hardware you can choose to add the new speaker drivers. Select a generic brand of speaker from the list and click install. That is a technique leaned from on the job experience, to know specifically that the speaker drivers are very easy to install and one driver fits all.
4. Change the properties of the currently installed speaker. Within the control panel you can choose the option for speakers and sound, and play around with the properties specific to your device. In one client's home I found that the settings were set to back, but the computer only plays sound when the speakers are set to front. At another client's home the client had purchased new speakers and had two sets of drivers installed. I had to change the default preference to play from the new speakers.

If your client needs a sound card repaired or otherwise replaced, refer your client to the local J & R Computers, Office Depot or Staples to have the part replaced. This is my rule of thumb that I always follow never to take apart a computer tower in the client's home. It creates too many instances of possibly having a hazard. We are only a computer tech otherwise charging an easy $40 minimum fee for our site visit and are not looking for any law suits.

Now as a computer tech one nice bonus to add is **iTunes.com** for downloading internet radio. My site fee is $40 check or cash and do not like to have any work take less then 15 minutes, so if you simply just plug in the speakers and get checked and walk out the door, spend the time to install **iTunes.com** and make sure that the computer gets the radio signal.

It was quickly determined that the speakers needed to be plugged into the green port, which is the middle port. After clicking on the Control Panel to determine the sound was working by clicking on, test the speakers, arrow symbol to hear them play; your day of work is just about done. It is time to ask the client for the $40 for the site fee, kick back and go out the local bar in time for happy hour, but following my principle of giving the client an extra tune up.

1. **iTunes.com** is already installed and you have tested out the comedy channel broadcast of Sara Palin's inauguration which otherwise never happened.
2. The speaker drivers are up to date.

Now there are two nice points to work on. I brought twist tie cables with me to organize the cables underneath the computer desk. When adjusting all of the cables accordingly a few of them needed to be tied into groups of three to prevent tangles of wires. This is called power management and is very helpful to peoples homes to have neat cables for extra leg room under there desks.

Done! We have gone above and beyond tying those cables together and there is nothing left based on this site call other then getting a check and going to the bank.

Example 2: A client complains that his internet is blocked because of a virus.

You get to the client's home and see an anti-virus pop-up with no subscription.

There are a few thing to check before you proceed.

1. Make sure the internet is plugged in. Check the TCP/IP connection located in the lower right corner of the screen and make sure that the failure is not that the cable is unplugged.
2. Ask your client of he has an anti-virus subscription
3. Ask your client if he owns a back-up USB drive for backing up his data.
4. Check the Windows XP machine to make sure that the OEM sticker is on the machine. This will be needed if the computer has a virus.

You got up to the Anti-virus screen and could not proceed any further without buying anti-virus. Ask your client for his card number and order the anti-virus software online.

Once the download completes, run the setup and install anti-virus on the system.

A few recommended anti-virus software's are:

1. AVG Anti Virus
2. Spybot Search and Destroy
3. McAfee (The most recommended)
4. Norton
5. PC Cilin

Download and setup the anti virus. Perform a full system scan and see how many viruses there are on the machine. I recommend McAfee because it is very reliable and you almost never get a call back asking you why the system has failed. It costs your client a little more money than expected but he will have a license that can be used on up to three computers. You finished the virus scan and the internet turned back on and your client's call was complete. $60 for the flat fee.

Example 3: The same client calls you back because he wants to get his hard drive better organized.

You arrive at the client's home and his internet is working fine. He asks you how to delete the extra icons on his desktop and get his files backed up more neatly.

Right mouse click on the icons you want to get rid of and click delete. Tell your client he must order a back-up USB drive in order to protect his data.

A few good web sites to buy a USB drive are:

1. **NewEgg.com**
2. **TigerDirect.com**
3. **BesBuy.com**
4. **JR.com**
5. **Amazon.com** Yes, Amazon has lots of computer parts

By the time you check the prices on all five of these web sites you will get the best deal.

Now your appointment is over until the hard drive arrives. Offer your client some extra bonuses while you are there. Clean the icons out of the start menu. Clean the icons out of the system tray. Ask your client which programs he would like to get rid of and delete them one at a time from the programs list. Deleted unwanted folders in the my documents folder. The last step is to run DEFRAG.EXE for your client to make sure his system is up to speed. Click Start/ All Programs/ Accessories/ System Tools and choose Defragment. Your day of work is done. Charge your client the $60 for the flat fee.

Example 4: This is your third and last visit to this client's home. You arrive and he shows you his new USB hard drive.

You plug in the hard drive and ask your client where he keeps his extra documents. You are directed not only to the documents folder but also the music and videos folders. By clicking copy and paste you copy all of the files into the new drive.

Label the drive for your client. You must keep your client's work space organized.

Offer your client a nice place to store his drive. Many of them just leave the drive out on there desk. Remind your client that he cannot get his drive wet or dirty with food or it will not work anymore.

As a little bonus label your clients back-up C.D.'s Almost all of them will have old C.D.'s lying around. Bring along a Sharpie marker and label each disk one at a time.

I bring with me extra C.D. carrying cases. There are common enough to find them at the 99 cents store. These neat C.D. cases make all the difference in the world when it comes to organizing old C.D.'s.

It took three appointments to this client's home but you are done. Leave the client your business card charge the last bill of $60 and move along your way.

Example 5: You get a call from a client saying that his hard disk failed and his laptop will not turn on. This system has a recovery partition.

Ask your client over the phone which version of Windows he has and bring to the appointment the correct C.D. I would recommend bring along an extra USB hard drive to the appointment to back-up all of his data on the first visit.

You arrive at the client's apartment and turn on his laptop. It gets a Windows error that a inf file is missing or corrupt.

You must recover all of the data and then only after recovering the data restore the operating system from the recovery partition.

Steps to follow:

1. Insert the recovery C.D.
2. Follow the on screen instructions to get the system booted.
3. Once Windows is turned on immediately back-up all of the data in the 'My Documents' folder as well as other files your client wants to hold onto.
4. Once you are certain everything is backed up, click on the Start/ Help/ recovery Partition/ Restore My Partition to an Earlier Time
5. Once the recovery partition is finished running, you will be able to restart Windows.
6. Make sure Windows starts without an error message

Charge your client the $60 for your hours spent. The next example we cover system reformat.

Example 6: You arrive at a client's home and he has backed up all of his data onto a disk already but does not know how to install Windows.

You check the system yourself and it does in fact have a lot of virus and pop-up's. You decide to reformat the computer.

Steps to follow for reformat:

Before getting started, go to the Manufacturers web site and download the drivers needed for your system. Remember after a reformat all of the drivers are deleted. You must have the drivers on a back-up USB.

1. Turn on the system and insert your Windows C.D.
2. Restart the computer and you will be taken to a screen that says press any key to start Windows.
3. You are prompted through a bunch of screens and then asked to delete the old partition. Once deleting the old partition, create a new partition.
4. The Windows setup begins and you are prompted to select a language, select English.
5. A few screens later you will be asked what time zone you are in.
6. The system will run through a few more steps and you will be asked for the OEM from the Windows Authenticity Sticker. Look on the bottom of the computer and type in the 20 digit OEM number.
7. Once the system turns on immediately activate Windows. Your client will not know to do this on his own. You must activate Windows and validate the OEM.
8. Insert the drivers USB drive and install each driver one at a time. Starting with the Chipset and Rom. Next Graphics and Modem drivers. Followed by drivers for the wireless network card. Last but not least drivers for the sound.

This appointment is done. A reformat should not take more than one hour and thirty minutes. Bill your client $60 and you are done.

Example 7: You get a call from a client who does not own a wireless router. He uses the near by connection but it is very slow.

Before your appointment go to J&R or Staples and buy a LinkSYS router. They range between $60 - $100. When arriving at the client's house check the connection to make sure the apartment has cable or DSL internet.

Steps to take to install the router:

1. Take the router out of the box and attach it to the cable router.
2. Once the router powers on check on laptop for s signal. You should see LinkSYS appear.

You are done. For setting a wireless password see the next example.

Example 8: You get a call from a client that has a wireless connection and does not know how to set a password. Confirm with your client that he has cable or DSL internet and already owns a LinkSYS.

For this kind of service call I recommend you serve your client over the phone. Open up your credit card terminal and charge your clients card $60 for the call.

You must follow the following steps with your client:

1. Ask your client to open his internet explorer and type in the URL 192.168.1.1
2. A screen comes up asking for the password the username by default is admin and the password is admin
3. You will be taken to the next screen asking for the name of the SSID. Ask your client to decide on an SSID and a password.
4. Click save.

You are done. Ask your client to test the connection by logging into the router with his Network and Sharing Center to test and make sure everything connects. You already made $60 today and you didn't even leave your home.

Example 9: You got a call from the owner of a Mac computer. He would like a wireless router set-up in his Manhattan apartment that connects to his Mac. For this call instead of a LinkSYS router we will use a NetGear.

You ask that the client go to Staples and buy a NetGear router before you come over. When you arrive you check and make sure the cable internet is working. Up until this point he always had his desktop G4 Mac connected with an RJ-45 connector but his wife's laptop never had internet in their tiny Manhattan apartment.

You follow these steps to get the router working:

1. Plug the router into the cable internet jack
2. Go onto the Desktop computer and run the NetGear C.D.
3. Follow the steps of setup and you will be prompted to set an SSID and password for the router
4. Once you have completed these steps the router should be ready for use.
5. Log onto the laptop and search for the router's name in the wireless connections. The name should appear on the list.
6. Type in the new password for the router and you are done.

Make sure your client has the password written down in a safe place. Bill the client $60. You are done for the day.

Example 10: A client calls you with a complaint that ever since he installed an unlicensed pirated copy of a software on his computer his system crashes and he gets pop-up messages.

For this service call we are going to use a Trojan scanning software. It is easy to find a good recommendation by going to c-net and typing in spyware under programs. Spyware scanning software runs about $30 per license.

Follow these steps to get rid of the spyware.

1. Run the spyware utility and scan the entire hard drive for bugs.
2. Once the scan is complete delete the bugs and remove them to the quarantine.
3. Open the control panel and open Add/ Remove Programs option.
4. Ask your client to name all of the software he has installed recently and delete them one at a time.
5. Restart the computer and all of the bugs should be gone.

A nice extra for your client is to install McAfee Anti-Virus and setup a firewall to protect the computer from intrusions. He will most definitely agree to pay the small fee for the McAfee license.

You are done. Bill your client $60 and you are on your way.

Example 11: You get a call to go work on a college campus for a few weeks. While working in the administrative offices one of the staff asks you to check that his system is working before his 2pm teleconference.

The staff member has a Dell computer with built in speakers and a web cam.

You test the speakers and they do not play any sound. You must go through the following steps to get the speakers working:

1. Open the Control Panel and click sound. Click on the drivers tab to make sure the driver is installed ok.
2. Check to see that the speakers are attached correctly and plugged in. This is the most common reason for no sound.
3. Using the control panel play a test sound to see if everything is working. They should be fixed by now.
4. Plug in the web cam and turn them on. Test that the web cam is recording.

Notify your client that his speakers are working and he can have his conference this afternoon.

Example 12: You get called to work on several old computers. You must diagnose the machines and figure out why they are not working.

Both of the machines are Dell Inspiron and both are not able to turn on.

You test each computer using the following steps:

1. Press the power button and see if the computer turns on.
2. If the computer does not turn on, write down any error message it may display.
3. If the power does not work at all, open each computer with a screw driver and look around inside. Check to see the memory sticks are in place, the hard drive and power supply are plugged in. Make sure all of the connections are plugged in tightly.

The first computer displayed the error message 'No Disk Found' You decided that the computer needed a new hard drive. By going to **Dell.com** and ordering a new Inspiron Hard drive using the campus on site warranty the first computer was taken care of.

The second computer had a lot of dust inside of the tower and basically just needed a cleaning. You used a mini vacuum cleaner and cleaned out all of the junk from inside. After putting the computer tower back together it was able to turn back on.

Example 13: It is the last week of classes on campus and a student approaches you with a question that he has installed Office 2007 and needs to display his word count to finish his paper.

You ask the student to bring his laptop to your office. You check Office 2007 and it does not have word count on any of the text editing features. Office 2003 displays the Word count right under the tools pull down. The student also complained that he had trouble finding spell check and he needed his computer back to normal to finish his final exams.

The answer is simple. All of the students are covered by the campus software license. You take out an old Office 2003 C.D. You install the older version of Office and restart the computer.

The student thanks you and goes on his way back to writing his paper with the Office tools he is accustomed to.

Example 14: The semester is over and you are back at your home office. You get a call by two business men that work downtown to come into their office and help them setup six laptops for new employees.

All of the laptops must have their user permissions restricted to only being able to browse the internet and take care of basic functions. You do not want any user installing new programs or making changes to the start up icons.

You log into each computer one at a time as the administrator. You go to Start/ Control Panel/ User Accounts and add a password to the administrator account. Make sure to give a copy of the password to the boss for future reference. On each machine you create two new limited accounts. You select to leave the password turned off.

You charge the boss $60 for the first three hours and your day is done.

Example 15: You get called back to work in the same office again and are asked to install and configure a voice over I.P. software that dials numbers for the telemarketers.

Follow these steps to install the VoIP software:

1. Log into each computer as the administrator and install the software. Select to have the software accessible by all users on the computer, not just administrators.
2. Once the software is installed double click the software icon to start the new program. You are taken to a screen that asks for the Mac address and IP of each station. These machines are running over a VoIP business phone service. The Mac address is typed on the back of each IP Phone on each desk in the office. Type in the Mac address one at a time and set the software to detect the IP automatically.
3. Repeat these steps on all six machines.
4. Run a test of the software to make sure they are working properly and get sound.

Your day is done. Charge the boss another $60 and you are on your way.

Example 16: You get called over to this office again and are asked to help the boss get his scanner scanning in PDF mode.

You check his system and while he does have a standard Cannon scanning software installed he does not have a software that creates PDF documents. Follow these steps to get his system working:

1. Go to **OpenOffice.org** and install the latest PDF writer software. This will only take a few moments to download and has all of the PDF capabilities you need.
2. Once the software is setup, perform a test scan of a document and save the document as a .doc
3. Open the document using Open Office Writer and save the document as a PDF.

This will get you working up to speed. If your boss has any extra questions about compression or embedding fonts, direct him to buy a copy a Adobe Acrobat Professional including Adobe Distiller or these days you can get Nuance Create PDF 6.

Your work for the day is done. A quick PDF install and you are already done. Isn't the life of a P.C. Technician an easy one? You charge the boss $60 and get on your way.

Example 17: You got a call from a client complaining that his computer has a pop-up saying "Warning Virus Detected"

You arrive to the client's home and he is using Windows 7 on his P.C. The pop-up message says that there is a virus and the user must purchase a copy of Anti-MalWare. It even displays a bunch of messages at startup. You try and delete the program using add remove programs but that is blocked. You must manually delete the program.

1. Right click on the program icons in the system tray and turn them off one at a time.
2. To locate the program in the hard drive press 'CTRL-ALT-DELETE' and the task manager will start. Look for the program name in the Task Manager and right click on the item. It will display the name of the folder that the program is located.
3. Browse to C:\Users\User Name\App Data and browse to the folder you are looking for. Click on the program and all of the files in the folder and click delete.
4. Empty the recycle bin as these programs are contaminated with a virus.
5. Run a virus scan as well as a spy ware scan and delete any unnecessary data.
6. Restart the computer one time and make sure the program does not start again

You are done. Good day of work. Charge your client the $60 and you are on your way.

Example 18: You get a call from a business in your neighborhood that an old computer and wants to upgrade the memory chip.

You get over to the location and the client first asks you what is the best way to speed the computer up. Looking at the fact that he needs at least 256 MB for his system requirements but only has 128 you recommend memory.

You must determine what kind of memory his system needs in order to proceed. Follow these steps to order the correct memory:

1. Look up the brand name of the computer in this case HP and go to the manufacturers web site **www.HP.com**
2. Click on Support & Drivers and browse to the correct model number you are looking for.
3. Ask your client for his credit card and order him several memory chips, one for each socket. The web site will say the maximum amount of memory possible to be allocated.
4. Double check with your client a date you can come back and install the new memory chips.

You are done for the day. The new memory is coming in the mail. Charge your client $60 and go to your next appointment.

Example 19: The client from the same store calls you when the new memory arrives. You get your Phillips head screw driver and laptop repair kit ready for use.

When arriving at the clients address he shows you the new box of memory that has arrived. Follow these steps to safely install the new memory chip:

1. Unplug the computer and make sure there is no static electricity.
2. Bring the computer into the back room of the store away from the customers.
3. Open the tower cover using your Phillips head screw driver.
4. Also make sure there is no extra static electricity in the interior of the machine.
5. Locate the old memory chips and remove them from the computer.
6. Take the new memory chips and click them into place one at a time.
7. Screw back on the cover of the tower.
8. Plug in the computer and make sure that the system powers up.
9. Check the MS-DOS screen and make sure the memory counts all the way up to 1,024 where it is supposed to.
10. Make sure that Windows starts like normal.

You are done. Charge the client $60. You now made $120 charging your client for two appointments to get done one memory job.

Example 20: You went to your clients location and he complained that his internet explorer cannot open PDF links.

Many computers do not come with Adobe Acrobat installed. Follow these steps to accommodate your client to get him a license from Adobe:

1. Check that there is no previously installed PDF writer software.
2. Go to **Adobe.com** and download Adobe Acrobat Reader.
3. Install the Adobe Flash Player as well.

You are already done. As a little extra ask the client of he owns a license to Adobe Acrobat Reader. If the answer is yes, accommodate the client by installing Adobe Acrobat Professional for him.

If your client does not own a copy of Adobe Acrobat order him a license from **Adobe.com** which runs around $199.00 If he is stuck over the price order him a copy of Nuance Create PDF or find a different version of the software by going to **Cnet.com** and browsing around.

Complete the download of the professional version of Acrobat. Install and register the software for your client.

You are done. Charge your client $60 and you are on your way.

Example 21: You get a call from a client that he needs to create PDF documents from Word. The client does not use his home printer. He makes PDF and Word docs and prints them in Manhattan.

You arrive at the clients home and check on his printer connections looking for a PDF output option. He does not have one. You must follow these steps in order to make PDF a printing option:

1. Go to **Adobe.com** and order your client a copy of Adobe Acrobat Professional.
2. Once downloaded ask your client for his credit card reminding him that he will be billed $199.00 and order him a copy of the latest Adobe Acrobat Professional.
3. Register the software under your clients name and email.
4. Restart the computer one time.
5. Once the computer powers up click on Start/ Printers or Start/ Devices and Printers.
6. Right mouse click on the Adobe icon and set th connection as the default printer.
7. Start Microsoft Word and run one test print to make sure that PDF is selected as the default.

As a nice extra: Save the newly purchased software registration as a PDF document and leave it on the desktop for your client to view later on.

You are done. Charge your client $60 and be on your way.

Example 22: You get a call from a client that he has a number of attachments in his email account that he cannot open.

You go over to the client's home and the documents are both .zip and .rar files. You must follow these steps in order for your client to be able to read the documents:

1. Go to **WinZip.com** and purchase a license for WinZip. It costs in the range of $29.95 and up.
2. Once the download is complete register the software with the newly purchased serial number and activate the software for full use.
3. Open the email software and click on the attachment that your client was trying to open. The file should open right away.

You are already done. Here are some extras to make your time more enjoyable.

Give your client a tutorial on how to use the WinZip software. Show your client how to create a new folder each time he unzips a document.

Many clients that email zip files also use ftp. Ask you client if he is familiar with ftp. Go to the web site, **CuteFTP.com** and order your client a copy of Cute FTP Professional. Download and register the software under your clients name.

Now you are done. Charge your client $60 and be on your way.

Example 23: You get a call from a client asking you why his Microsoft Word Cannot open a word document he received by attachment.

You arrive at the client's home and find out it was not a .doc file but in fact a .docx file. The remedy for this is your client must purchase a version of Office 2007 or later.

1. You direct the client to **Microsoft.com**
2. Browse to the Office Section of the web site. You will see the latest versions of Office offered.
3. Purchase your client a copy of Office 2007 or later. Depending on your clients needs he may need more than the standard Office Home Edition. If he needs to use database features included with Access or create interactive presentations with PowerPoint then Home Edition may be the wrong choice.
4. Register the software under your client's name and email.
5. Save a copy of the software registration as a PDF document onto your clients desktop. For Microsoft products this includes the registration key. Your client will need this key if he wants to keep his license some time later in the future.

We are already done, but I always offer extras. After all we are charging the client $60 for up to three hours. Show your client how to use Microsoft Web App's Browse to **Microsoft.com** and click on Office or as a more direct approach go to **Office.Live.com** or **OfficeLive.com** and browse to Web App's. This is a great way for clients to look for specific office features that they will buy in the future.

Charge your client $60. You are done for the day.

Example 24: You get a call asking how to turn her contacts list into an excel spread sheet. Your client has several different email accounts all needing to be converted.

You try to work with the client over the phone but she is a senior, disabled, and needs your help in person. You make it over to the client's house and familiarize her with the difference between .xls and .csv Sitting down with the client you follow these steps to get going:

1. Log into each hotmail account one at a time and click on Contacts/ Manage/ Export You will be asked what format select .xls
2. Do the same for her free aol and other emails.
3. Open Microsoft Excel and open each spread sheet one at a time.
4. Copy and paste the bottom of the first sheet onto the top of the second sheet and repeat these steps until all of the contacts are in one sheet.

You are done. Show the client where email and phone number fields are located on the excel sheet. As an extra bonus open Microsoft Outlook and Import all of the excel sheets into the Microsoft Excel contacts book. Show your client how to start Outlook each time she wants to resume her telephone campaign.

Charge your client $60. You are done for the day.

Example 25: You get a call from a senior citizen that she is locked out of her Aol account. Even worse, her wireless internet stopped working. She is using a Mac laptop in her house. You try to fix her problem over the phone but with no luck. The internet is not working.

Once arriving at the client's home she showed you her laptop with no connection. She has Hughes net for her wireless service.

1. You check and confirm that the router is turned on.
2. Check the wireless connections on the laptop. Sure enough, she was logged into a different SSID.
3. You go to Aol and ask your client to type in her user name and password. You get an error message WRONG PASSWORD
4. You instruct your client to click the forgot password button, type in her secret answer birth date and name.
5. Have her type in her new password.
6. Instruct your client to write the password down in a safe place.

You charge your client $60. Nice easy day of work. Many days are like this working with seniors. They have difficulty with basic computer tasks and often need the help of an IT Technician.

Example 26: You get a call from a business person. He just bought a Blackberry device and needs to be able to check his email.

You arrive at your clients office and he has a new Blackberry, indeed, with no email accounts added. Follow these steps to add email accounts, one at a time:

1. Browse to email and click setup
2. You will be prompted for what kind of email service HTTP, POP3 or IMAP in this case your client has POP3.
3. You type in the ingoing POP3 and outgoing SMTP server addresses. Make sure to use the correct server address each email service provider has a different one.
4. You will be asked for the user name and password for the email account.
5. On some devices you will be asked to type in a display name for his clients to view when receiving his emails.
6. Go through these steps again for each additional email account your client would like to add. Many business men use at least one company email and one personal email.

You are done. As an extra bonus show your client how to download his emails to his laptop computer. The easiest way to do this is go to Microsoft.com and search for the current outlook connector. There are different versions of the connector depending on what kind of device your client is using. Just search for Blackberry POP3 download and you will be directed to many resources. There is a different connector for your clients Blackberry than a Pocket P.C.

Charge your client $60. You are on your way.

Example 27: You get a call from a client who wants to download and archive all of the photos from her new digital camera.

Before going to the client's house you stop by the local Staples and buy a real of blank C.D.'s This is essential to keeping your client happy, being prepared to create a backup. The last thing you want is a canceled job because you need to make an extra trip to the computer store and your appointment is canceled. You will also need a permanent felt tip marker. Also include a nice C.D. holder in case your client does not already have one.

1. Attach the USB cable to the back of the digital camera.
2. Turn on your client's laptop and plug in the digital cameras USB cord.
3. You will be prompted to download the photos onto the hard drive and asked weather to delete the old ones from the camera. Ask your client if she would like to keep the photos or not. In this case she wants to download the photos but keep many of them but not all of them on her camera.
4. Once the photos are downloaded into the pictures folder take out a blank C.D. and burn the files onto disk. Label the C.D. and put the C.D. into the holder.
5. Browse to the C: drive and open up the directory for the digital camera.
6. Sit with your client and delete the unwanted photos one at a time.
7. Once you are done, empty the computers recycle bin.

You are done. Make sure to be reimbursed for the C.D.'s and the holder. Give your client the receipt from Staples. Charge your client $60 and you are done for the day.

Example 28: You get a call from a client. Every time she opens Picassa her computer freezes and her programs close down. You ask your client if she has a virus and her answer is no, but the computer is very old.

You arrive at the clients home and start Picassa and are taken to a screen with a large number of recently added video downloads. You check the file size of the videos and they are each close to 1GB. The outage is indeed caused by a memory failure.

1. You remove the video from the menu selection and close Picassa.
2. You restart Picassa and the video no longer appears.
3. You client needs to keep the video for her job but wants the video deleted from her computer. You take out one blank D.V.D. and burn the video for safe keeping. The D.V.D. takes about 15 minutes to burn and there are several. Do not forget that if our job takes more than 3 hours we charge $20 per additional house. Burn each video onto D.V.D. one at a time and label them each with your felt tip marker.
4. Restart the computer and then start Picassa.
5. This is time consuming but help your client organize her photos. Right mouse click on the photo selection and browse to the directory they are saved on the hard drive.
6. Burn the photos onto C.D. without being asked. You are the professional and backup is one of the primary job functions of a practicing IT.
7. Make sure your client has the latest version of Picassa installed.

As an extra bonus put all of the C.D.'s and D.V.D.'s into a holder. Also ask your client if she would like you to stay extra and backup her My Documents folder. If she insists everything is OK remind your client she may have a virus and she must backup all of her documents right away. As one more extra take out one of your unused copies of anti virus on disk and run a virus scan.

Make sure to be reimbursed for the C.D.'s D.V.D.'s holder and anti virus disk. Charge your client $60 plus $20 per hour extra for the appointment. It was a long day but data backup is not easy and is one of the reasons we are paid so much as IT Professionals.

Example 29: You are speaking with a long standing client and she says she finally got her software setup with her photo viewer, PDF page maker, music player, extra software for her web cam, and everything the way she always wanted it to be. You urge your client to make a Ghost of her operating system and insist that she make an appointment with you. She will not regret it.

Before going to this appointment you pick up one extra USB external hard drive. You arrive at the clients home and ask her to use her credit card to purchase a copy of Norton Ghost.

1. She purchases one Norton Ghost download and you install the ghosting software on her system.
2. Plug in the new USB hard drive.
3. Start the Ghost and you will be prompted for which drive to save the files. Select the external USB.
4. When Ghost starts you will be asked which part of the system to Ghost, either the Operating System, the Operating System and Software, or the Operating System, Software and My Documents files and folders as well. Choose the third option. You want to back up all of the files for your client. She may say that she has her documents on disk already but as an IT our primary job is data backup. Ghost the entire system and she will come back to thank you later.

The Ghost will take about 30 minutes to run. Double check on the USB once your are finished and make sure the files are all in one neat data packet. You are done. Charge your client $60 and go to your next appointment.

Example 30: You get a call from a store owner that needs his computer backed up once per week. He is running a Windows XP Operating System.

You go over to the client's store location and check for Ghosting software. He has none but he has standard Windows utilities. You check his hard drive and it is already divided into a 40 GB C drive and a 120 GB E drive. Follow these steps to schedule a weekly backup:

1. Click on Start/ All Programs/ Accessories/ System Tools and Click on the Task Scheduler.
2. Choose Backup. You will be prompted to choose how often select Weekly.
3. When asked what time of day, consult your client and find out what time he turns his computers on every Monday morning. You will be prompted for where to save the back up files, choose the D: drive and make a folder location to save the archives.
4. Perform the first backup manually while at the client location.
5. Check to make sure that the backup was successfully created on the D: drive.

You are done. As an extra, advise your client to buy an external hard drive. He may refuse but insist with your client that his hard drive will fill up very soon each backup being over 5GB and that he only has a matter of weeks. Order the external hard drive with your clients credit card. Charge your client $60 and on to yet another appointment.

Example 31: A client calls you saying he just bought a new laptop with Windows 7 and he needs to move all the files from his old computer using Windows XP. Your client already owns a USB hard drive.

You ask the client if he would like to keep the files or all of his settings as well. Your client insists that he uses Microsoft Office every day and he needs all of his office documents intact and all in a central location in his My Documents folder.

1. On the Windows XP machine go to **Microsoft.com** and download Windows easy transfer.
2. Run Windows Easy Transfer and get all of the files allocated from the My Documents folder into one easy to transfer archive.
3. Put the easy transfer archive onto the USB hard drive.
4. Connect a USB cable from the new Windows 7 laptop to USB hard drive.
5. On the Windows 7 laptop once again go to **Microsoft.com** and download Windows Easy Transfer. Start the program.
6. When prompted, browse to the archive on the USB disk and follow the prompts to restore the files.
7. Ask your client to take a look at his newly restored files to make sure everything is intact.

You are done. As an extra make sure your client keeps his archive saved. Many users may try and delete the archive once it is used to restore the new computer. While you are at it make one backup of the entire My Documents folder of the old computer onto the USB hard drive. Many clients do not notice until later that files are missing and our primary job as an IT is data backup.

Charge your client $60 and go to your next appointment.

Example 32: A client calls that he must backup his computer with a disk image and does not have a DVD burner. You previously ordered this client an external hard drive.

You check the client's system and he is running Windows 7 Ultimate. Familiar with Windows XP terms you perform a quick search on the help files and find a built in disk imaging by using 'Backup and Restore'

1. Click Start/ Help and Support
2. One the left panel click 'Create a System Image'
3. The next screen will ask where do you want to save your data click 'USB Drive' and the appropriate letter.
4. Let the backup run and create a disk image. They are no less than 25GB so make sure your USB Drive is up to standard.

Make sure your client knows not to delete his backup image and give a few pointers for safe hard drive storage. A book shelf in drawer is the best place for a USB Drive. Do not leave it on your desk.

Charge your client $60 and go on your way.

Chapter 3: Hiring a Writer.

So you have a nice set of credentials to fix computers and want to start advertising. Of course you do not want to write your ads on your own and the ones you made previously got flagged and removed from **CraigsList.com**

What do we do now?

Hire a writer.

Question: OK, I have hired a writer before, my Aunt Rachel, but no one replied to my ad and I even got complaints. What do I do now?

Answer: Your writer must be an English major. The local college is a great place to look. You can rely on your Aunt for advise and things but this is business. Hire a writer to have a professional ad.

Question: My writer does not know technology terms. I tried working with her several times on my text and she keeps changing around my Microsoft terms.

Answer: Work closely with your writer. Make sure your writer knows which terms you would like to keep and which terms were not necessary. As long as the writer knows that A+ certified is the actual name of your certificate and must be stated as a credential everything will be OK.

Question: I wrote my ad to my liking but it does not have any images. Where do I find some pictures I can use?

Answer: You must use some computer savy images including a Microsoft logo and other logo's and images to make your ad work. Also you may want to hire a designer to make you a nice set of computer repair icons, but I recommend simply searching on Google images for your computer key words and find an image that is nice.

Tip: Make a deal with a graphic designer to make you some graphics, in exchange you will find him a few extra clients. Make a space in your ad for Graphic Design. Have your designer pay you %10 of each client.

Chapter 4: Be Your Own Writer. Use a Template.

Before I used a template my ad had no structure. It read like a spool of text. I used a simple template I found on **ThumbTack.com** and the results were great. I had a completely formatted ad. Not only that but my callers were much easier to speak with about my services. Here is an example of an ad from **SkillSlate.com** Keep in mind the page is broken into the following categories…

1. Name
2. Web Site URL
3. Hourly Rate
4. Price Details
5. Availability
6. Business Information
   a. Type of Payments Accepted
   b. Services Offered
   c. Areas Served
   d. Available Weekends
   e. Free Consultation
   f. Examples of Past Work
   g. Licenses and Certifications
   h. Memberships and Associations
   i. Design Layout
7. Personal Information
8. Languages Spoken

The ad actually looked like this…

Peter Sloan, Graphic Designer

shopusanetwork.com
New York, NY
http://ShopUSAnetwork.com

Hourly Rate: $ 20.00 per hour

Price Details: Flat Fee as well

Peter Sloan's **Availability**

Mon	Tues	Wed	Thurs	Fri	Sat	Sun
9 AM to 9 PM	9 AM to 9 PM	9 AM to 9 PM	9 AM to 9 PM	9 AM to 9 PM	12 PM to 5 PM	12 PM to 5 PM

Peter Sloan's **Business Information**

Types of payment accepted:	Cash, Visa, Mastercard, Amex, Paypal
Services offered:	Illustration, Logo and Identity Design, Print Design, Print Design & Layout, Visual Design, Web Design
Areas served:	Manhattan
Available weekends:	Yes
Free Consultation:	No
Examples of Past Work:	http://shopusanetwork.com
Licenses and Certifications:	Adobe Certified Expert (ACE), CompTIA A+, CompTIA Net+, Dell Authorized Representative (DDET), Microsoft Certified Professional (MCP), Microsoft Certified System Administrator (MCSA), Microsoft Office Specialist (MOS)
Memberships and Associations:	Cooper Union Certificate, New Horizons C.L.C., S.U.N.Y. Purchase Alumni Association
Design Layout:	Brochure Design, Business Card Design , CD & DVD Covers, e-Catalog Design , Flyer Design, Identity Design , Logo Design, Magazine Layout Design , Newsletter Design , Packaging Design, Postcard Design, Web Design, Web Templates Design

Peter Sloan's **Personal Information**

Languages spoken:English

Remember Less is more. While we can have a slide show of images we do not want to add anything unnecessary. Here are a few sample images I used.

A chess piece drinking coffee, and a photo of my truck, but nothing else. Less is more. The customers want to read about computer credentials. They do not want to browse through some ones Face Book photo album.

Artist: Peter Sloan

Photo: Peter Sloan & Company

Your ad is done Copy and Paste it into the News Groups Bulletin Boars and CraigsList. If you cannot list on Craigslist there are tons of other web sites. Here are a few.

1. **CityListing.org**
2. **Fruzo.com**
3. **SkillWho.com**
4. **SuperShopper.org**

Write an article for your service and place it on **eZineArticles.com**

Post in the Google News Groups. You get so much exposure, heck that is why I have a book published today, **Google.com** News Groups, I have one for chess, **Rec.games.chess.misc** where I post links to my web sites and other information.

1. **Chapter 5:** Running a Classified Ad.

Now we have all of our text for our classified ad and we need to list ourselves. Here are some great places to get started.

1. **CraigsList.com**
2. **YellowPages.com**
3. **eBay.com** Classifieds, formerly **Kijiji.com**

Post your ad into all three of these sources.

Done. Easy. What is next?

Make a web site for your services. Reserve yourself a domain name and web site from Microsoft Office Live by visiting **OfficeLive.com** and signing for a free web site and documents storage space.

Still not done, order yourself a business card from **VistaPrint.com** Make sure it states your company name and web address. These days all professionals have a web site link on there card.

Chapter 6: Copyright Your Ad.

Submit your files for copyright and pay your $35 copyright registration fee online at **CopyRight.gov** Unless your copyright is disputed or has a legal problem $35 is the entire fee. Upload your copyright material online and hang tight. In 6 months you will receive a certificate like this…

Certificate of Registration

This Certificate issued under the seal of the Copyright
Office in accordance with title 17, *United States Code*,
attests that registration has been made for the work
identified below. The information on this certificate has
been made a part of the Copyright Office records.

Maria A. Pallante

Acting Register of Copyrights, United States of America

Registration Number

TX 7-316-875

**Effective date of
registration:**

November 11, 2010

Title

Title of Work: Peter Sloan Teaches How to Draw Cartoons

Completion/Publication

Year of Completion: 2010

Date of 1st Publication: August 3, 2010   **Nation of 1st Publication:** United States

International Standard Number: ISBN   1451598750

Author

■   **Author:** Peter Julius Sloan

Author Created: text, artwork

Citizen of: United States   **Domiciled in:** United States

Copyright claimant

Copyright Claimant: Peter Julius Sloan, dba Sloans Book Press

693 E 18th St, Brooklyn, NY, 11230, United States

Rights and Permissions

Name: peter julius sloan

Email: keno18nyc@aol.com   **Telephone:** 347-451-1154

Address: 693 east 18th street

brooklyn, NY 11230

Certification

Name: Peter Julius Sloan

Date: September 3, 2010

Correspondence: Yes

Page 1 of 1

46

Chapter 7: Registering Your Business Name.

This is a two step process. First we must make up a business name. If you change your business name you can always update this later.

1. Go to **IRS.gov** and search 'Get a Tax ID online'
2. Fill out the questions and you will be prompted to type in your new business name.

You will get your Tax ID online on screen that appears like this…

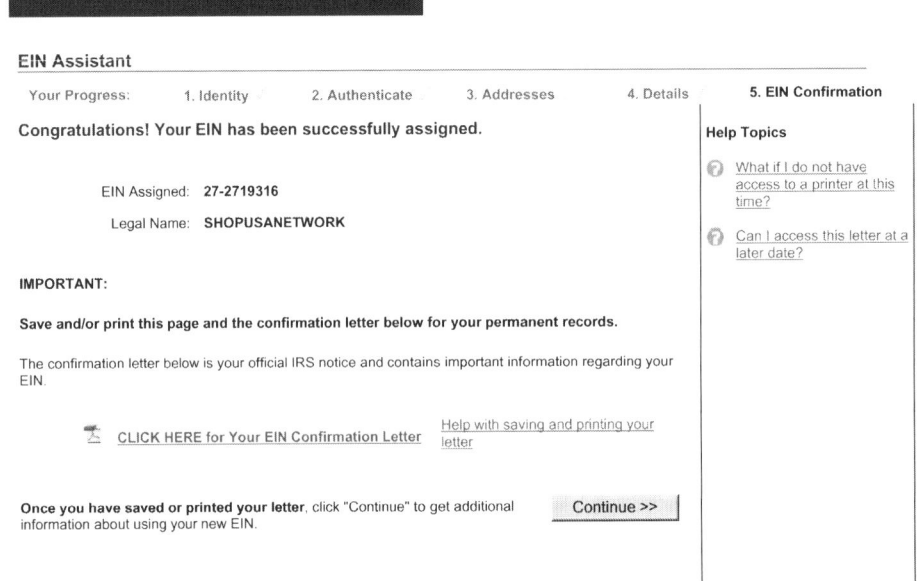

OK Great You have your Tax ID. Online the same day. Basically no one gets declined on a Tax ID unless they have a felony conviction so go online and get your Tax ID right now.

Step 2: Validate your Tax ID with your respective State Tax Office. Mine is New York.

Question: Does this mean I have to go stand on line downtown and go to the city clerk?

Answer: No. That is the old days. Now you can validate your Tax ID online paying a small fee and everything is done.

Great places to validate your Tax ID…

1. **InfoTaxSquare.com**
2. **IncFile.com**
3. **LegalZoom.com**

Pay your fee online to avoid the hassle. Less than two weeks later I got a certificate in the mail that looks like this…

Validated. Now we are in Business.

Chapter 8: Email Marketing Blast.

Send email to all of your contacts, weather they be alumni from school, people from your office, visitors to your local chess club, people that replied to your ad. All of these emails should be collected in one list and ready for an email blast. A few good services to choose from are...

1. **ConstantContact.com** , Recommended by President Obama
2. **SalesinaClick.com** for eBay pro stores
3. **iContact.com** Recommended by Microsoft

If you like writing short clips try **SafeMailServices.com** a great way to blast your online ad. I signed up for banner exchange with **PostYourAdz.com** I had to upgrade my membership for a small one time fee of $40 and I get a banner for my web site collecting new clients.

Make sure you have a permission to email your clients before you send out your blast. Make sure to remove all of the AOL addresses off your list before sending out your email or you will be reported as spam.

Here is a sample of how a new computer business email should look...

Let's start with a Banner. You must have a nice simple font with a computer related background. This background I took from **CompTIA.org** stationary and typed my company name over it.

Next you must prepare the body of your email. You want a simple clear message with a description of your services.

"2011 My new computer repair shop" "347-451-1154, Need a computer fix, call us today"

State your credentials, my credentials for IT read as follows,

Licenses and Certifications:	Adobe Certified Expert (ACE), CompTIA A+, CompTIA Net+, Dell Authorized Representative (DDET), Microsoft Certified Professional (MCP), Microsoft Certified System Administrator (MCSA), Microsoft Office Specialist (MOS)

PayPal buttons. I needed a way to charge my clients for over the phone consultations, because I get so many phone calls asking for free computer advice I came up with a nice ad for Coffee House Consultation and Telephone Computer Lessons.

The telephone lessons cost $20 per hour. It is a friendly way to say consultation but most of my clients are senior citizens so I went with the lessons angle many years ago.

Telephone Computer Lessons $20	Coffee House Consultation $35	Telephone and Internet Chess Lessons $20

Out of the three options above Coffee House Consultation requires that I leave my home so I charge at least $35 for the appointment.

You can place your phone number in bold text, and make it really big. You can also add a testimonial but that is about it. You ad is complete. Ready to send out to your readers.

Make sure to reinforce with every client that your time costs money. You do not want a voice mail box of 30 callers all asking you for free advice. Many people will get angry at first but the clients that are serious about learning there computer better will call you back all the time.

Chapter 9: Preserving Your Contacts.

So you are running your ad and get at least 10 new email addresses in your inbox every day. You must create a contacts book and backup your contacts with a Microsoft Excel spreadsheet.

Follow this simple formula to add all of your new recipients to your list:

1. Keep an email blast script in Microsoft Word format saved on your desktop.
2. For every contact that writes you copy and paste your script from Word into your email editor.
3. Once the email is sent you will be asked to add the contact to your address book. Type in the recipient's first and last name if you know it and save the contact.

Here is my sample email script…

Shop USA Network Web Site Design
347-451-1154
sales@shopusanetwork.net

Web Site Design 3 types
http://www.shopusanetwork.net/web-site-design.html

PowerPoint Web Sites $399

http://www.shopusanetwork.net/powerpoint-web-sites.html

Small Business Web Sites $575

http://www.shopusanetwork.net/small-business-web-sites.html

So we have sent one script of our services to every new email in our inbox. We clicked add to address book. We followed these steps for months, now it has been several years. We must backup our contacts book as an excel spreadsheet. Follow these steps:

1. In MSN, Hotmail, Office Live Click Manage/ Export
2. In Yahoo or Gmail click on the contacts tab and click to Export as well.
3. You will be asked to type in the verification text
4. Your contacts will be downloaded as a nice neat excel sheet.

I have all of my excel sheets stored like this...

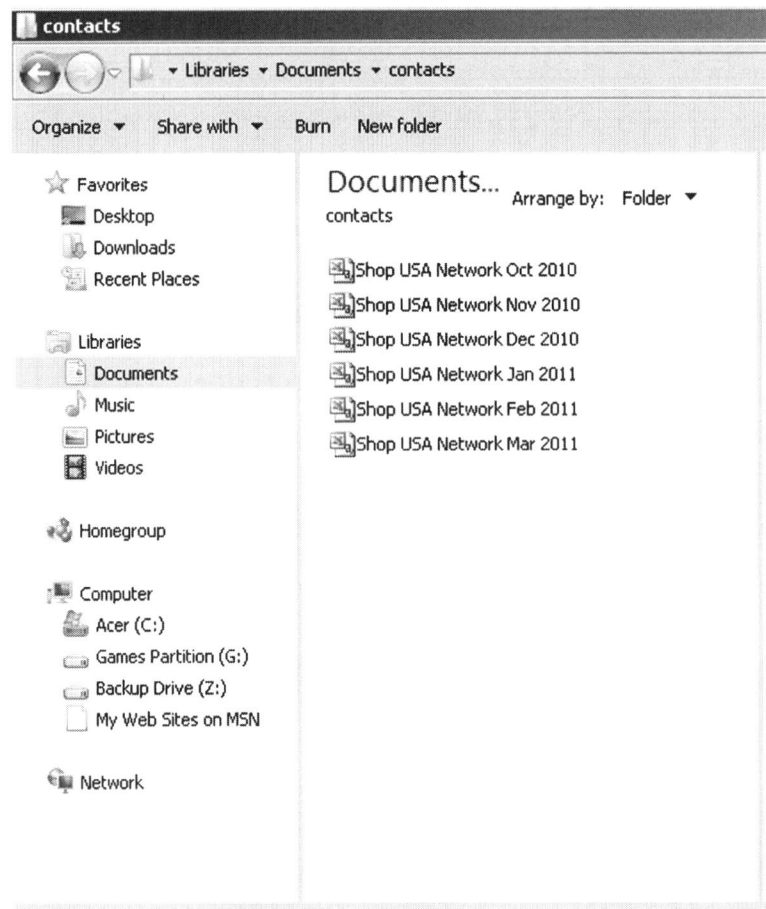

Is that all? Are we done? No way. No we are going to organize our, contact into a Microsoft Outlook Contacts Book where we can add clients phone numbers and addresses. We can also add secondary emails addresses to contact. While Outlook Express is free Microsoft Outlook is a very good investment in your money for a great way to organize your business.

Once you have your contacts ready as an excel spreadsheet open Outlook/ Click on the contacts tab and click File/ Import and Export

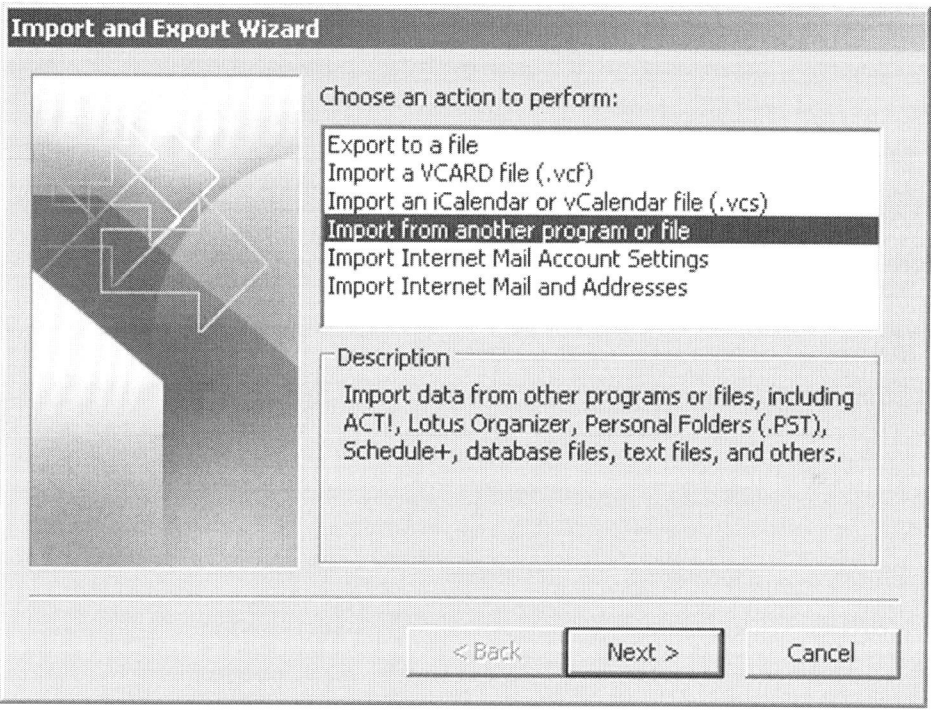

Since we already have our contacts Exported as an excel spreadsheet we will click 'Import from another program or file' If you wanted to Import straight from Hotmail Yahoo Business or Gmail you would select Import Internet Mail and Addresses.

The next screen will ask you what format you would like to import…

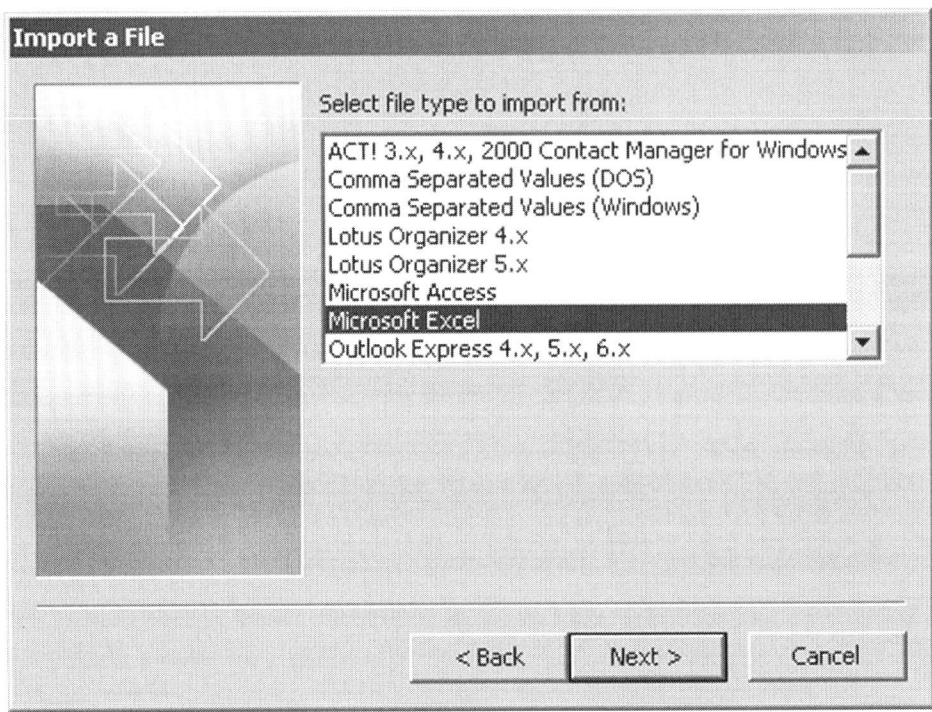

We have selected Microsoft Excel. The other popular option is Comma Separated Values .CSV Of course you can select Outlook Express for the free version.

The last screen will ask you to select a file from your hard drive. Browse to the file and select it from the list. In this example I am using Windows 7 so I will browse to Documents/ Contacts and select the appropriate spreadsheet.

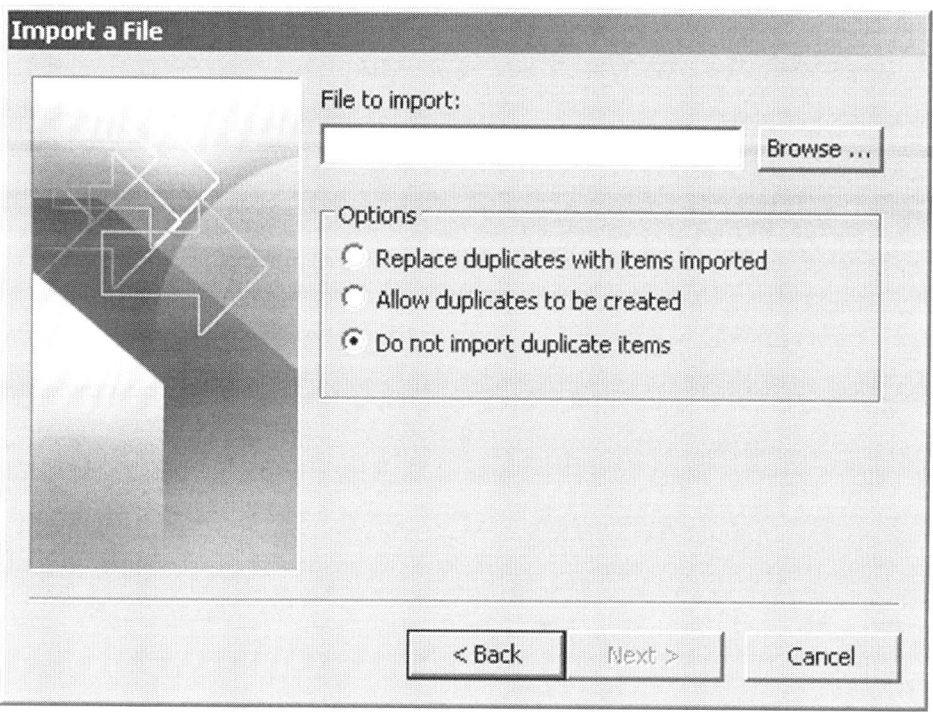

Select 'Do not import duplicate items if you are importing from the same email account more than once or importing several excel spreadsheets. It may be the case you want to import your spreadsheet file as often as once per month to capture all of your new contacts and leads in one place on your hard drive. Preventing duplicates is important.

For Mac Computers we do not use CSV format or Excel but instead VCard files. They are little index cards one for each contact. They are as easy to use as spreadsheets and in the event you switch over to Windows you see your VCards will be intact.

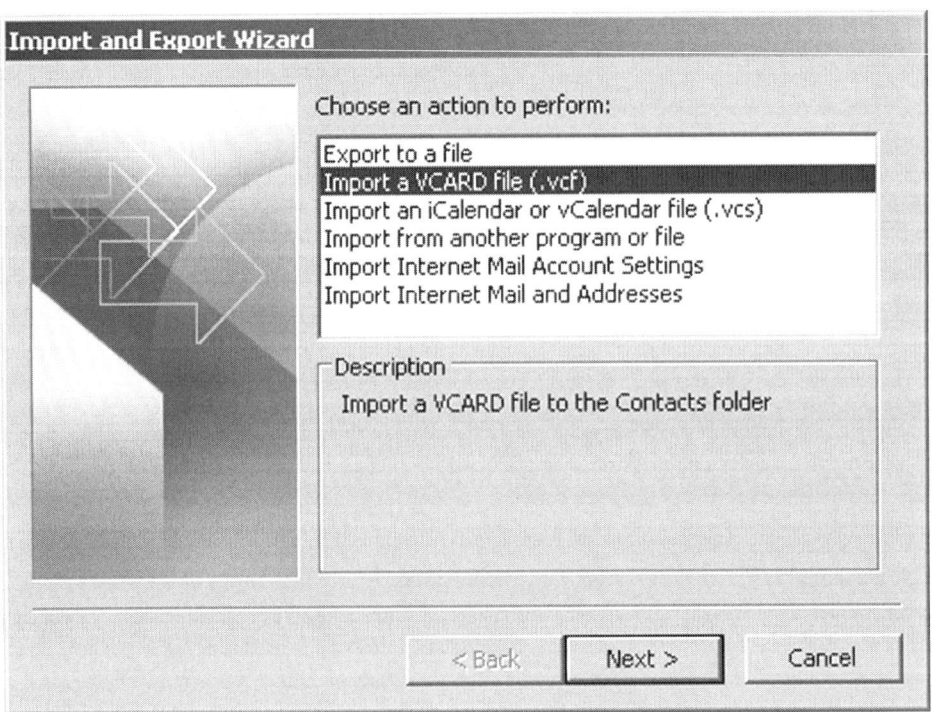

iCalendar and vCalendar files are also for Mac.

Done? We made an address book. Look, Mom, all done? No, not yet. Now we must make an archive for all of our emails being collected in our email account from our classified add. Making an email archive is extremely valuable and is the only way to protect communication with your clients. Simple leaving your emails around your inbox, even if they are in folders is not enough. You must backup your email box using Outlook. In the previous example we imported all of our contacts. Now we are going to download all of our emails into one neat .pst file.

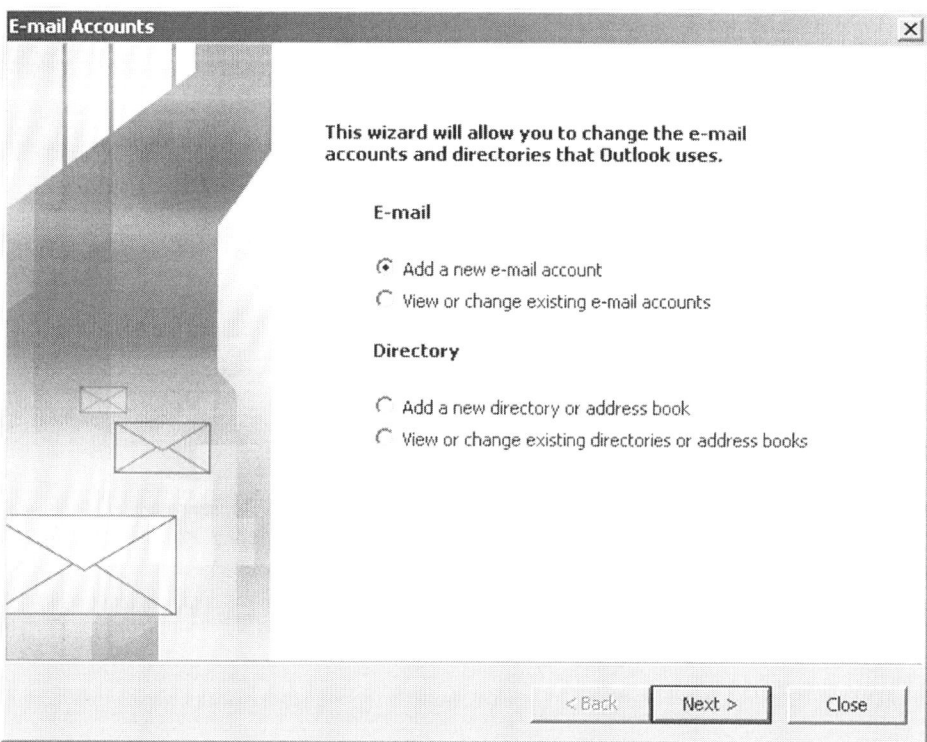

Select 'Add a new e-mail account. Making changes later on such as password or port numbers we will select 'View or Change existing e-mail accounts'

You will be asked what type of email server. For almost all of them select POP3. Some hosting providers use IMAP.

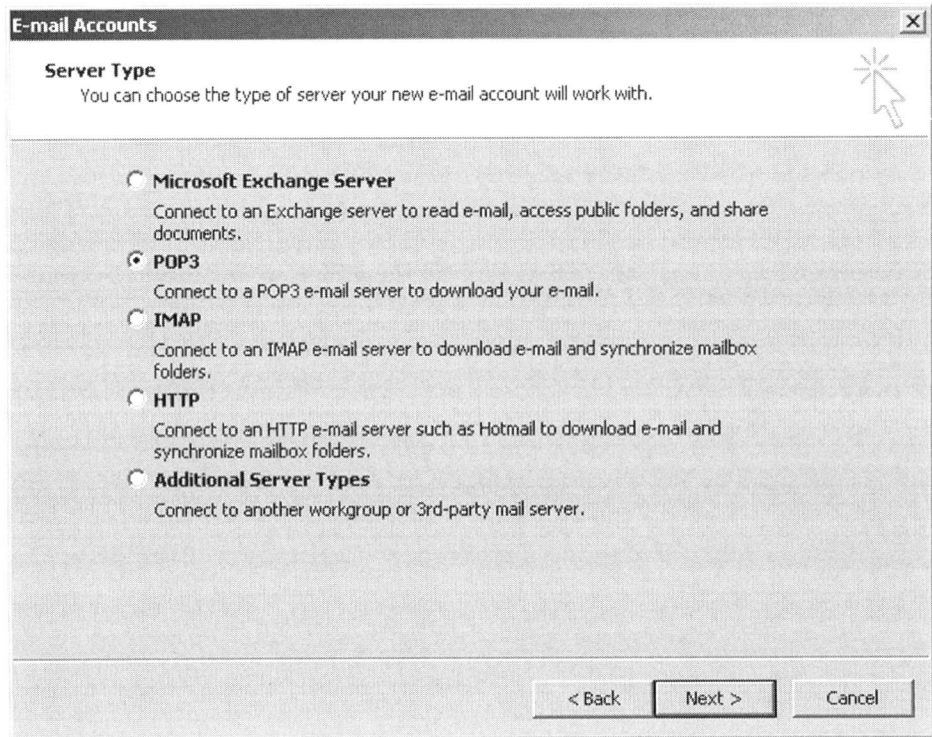

Of course you can set you Gmail account to download in HTTP but this is not necessary. POP3 is a nice universal form of downloading your email box onto your hard drive.

The configuring work is just about done. All you need to do is type in your user name, password, email address. Your POP3 Incoming and Outgoing mail server is different for every email service provider. Mail these days almost never uses SPA.

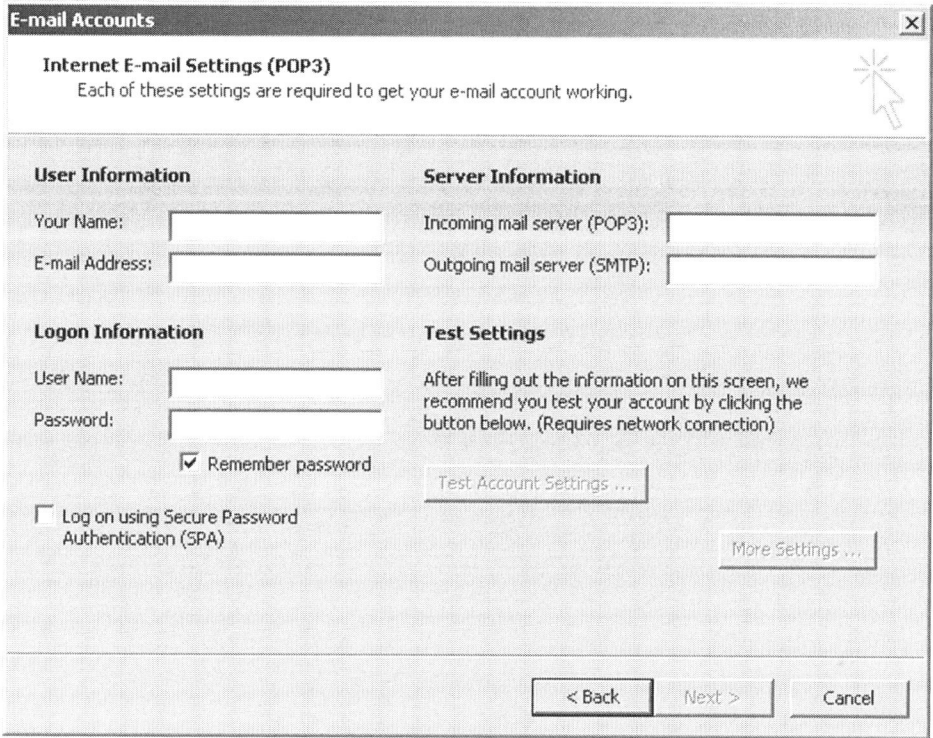

For Gmail you will also need to type in port numbers. These are located under more settings. When you are done adding your email account information click on 'Test Account Settings' and your Outlook will run a quick check to see if you are ready to download all of your email messages.

Now we have contacts and a hard copy of our email box. We have even organized nice neat folders shown below.

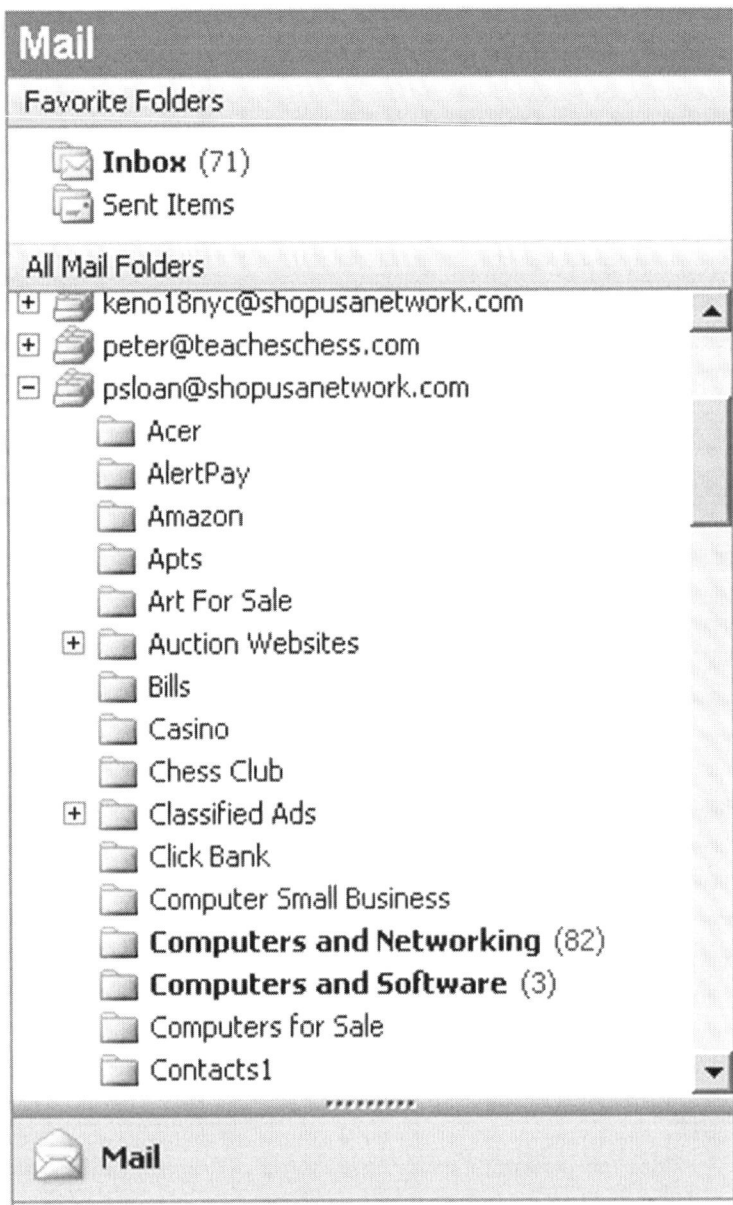

Now we are going to backup all of our email boxes into one .pst archive. This is as important as backing up all of your .xls or .csv spreadsheets. We create a backup following these steps.

Select the mail tab (Remember selecting contacts will allow you to export and backup your address book. In this case we are backing up our inbox.)

Select File/ Archive

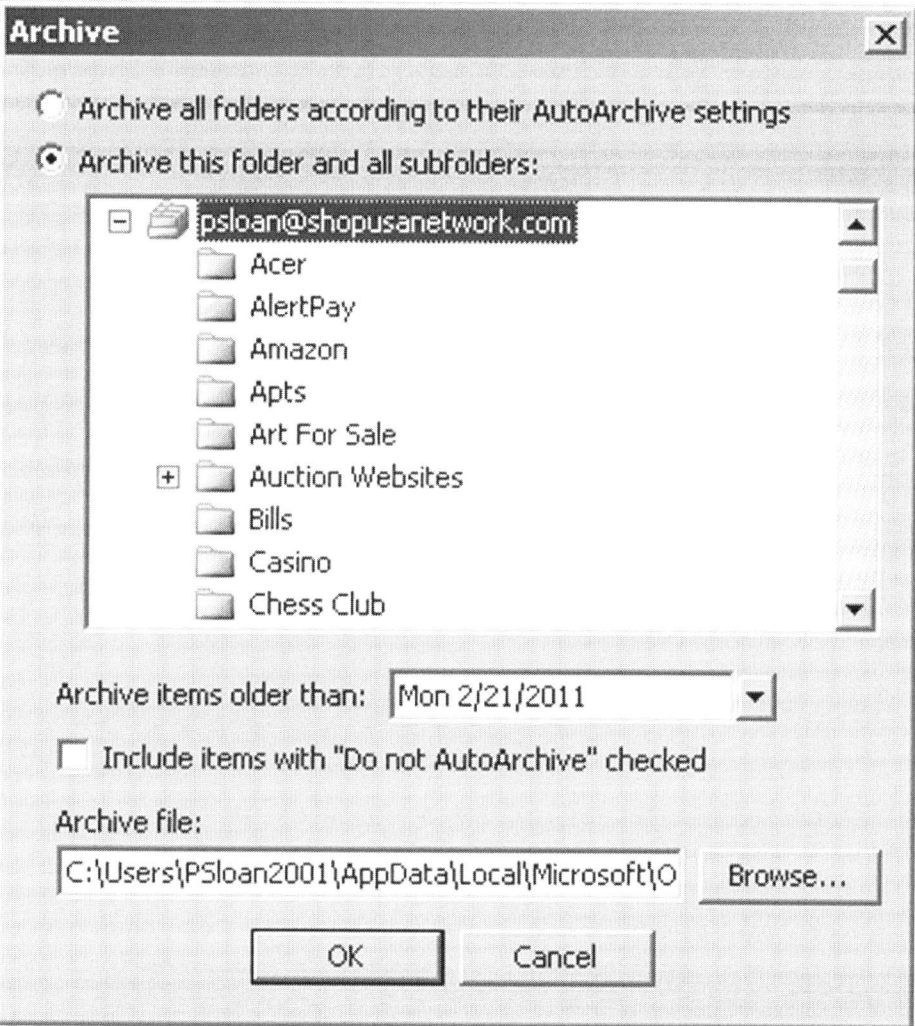

In the lower portion you are directed to where the archive file will be stored. Make a note of this, as soon as we archive the mail box we are going to make a backup copy onto a USB/ DVD.

Now in this case I browsed to C:\Users\PSloan2001\AppData\Local\Microsoft\Outlook\archive.pst folder which looked like this…

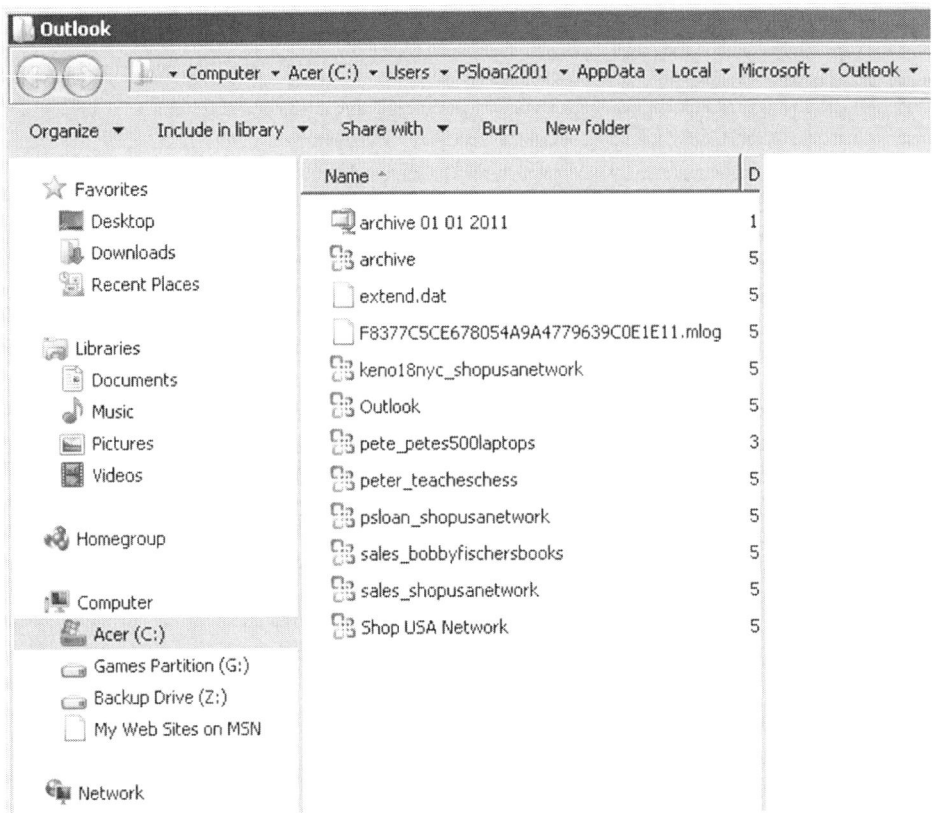

In Windows XP It would be located in C:\Documents and Settings\Psloan2001\AppData\Microsoft.

Burn all of the following documents onto a DVD or external USB drive. The archive is only a compressed version of your Outlook inbox. You must backup all of the following files for safe keeping.

Yes you can see, folks, I spent enough hours as a computer repair man that since the advent of all of these extra marketing devices I now spend more hours designing advertising campaigns than actually fixing broken computers.

That is where computers went for me. I am working as a Graphic Designer freelance for various publications, but not for the next person. One person I went to graduate school with got a job as an office IT servicing Windows 7 machines. The next person got hired assembling show case artwork for a local store. A friend from my office got noted for being good a Microsoft excel and was hired as a full time excel accountant and book keeper. My good friend from my bachelors, Sergio, sent out his ad for computer and house repair and got hired as the painting manager for a Manhattan office building, so we don't know where the email and contacts campaign is going to take us. Only time will tell.

Chapter 10: Accepting Payments Online/ by Phone.

PayPal is the most widely accepted form of online payments today. Of course you can get a Merchant Account from your local bank and accept Credit Cards and if you own a store front business, swiping cards in person every day is the best way to go, but for our purposes as freelance computer repair men with classified ad's and doing most business over the phone or at the client's site location, we must make PayPal our payment standard.

We all start with PayPal personal accounts. When you follow the advice in Chapter 7 Registering your business name and getting a Tax ID, we are now going to upgrade our PayPal accounts to Business. You will be sent a form from PayPal to verify your business Tax ID. You must sign and fax in this form to add your Tax ID to your PayPal account.

A few things to remember.

Configure all of your Buy Now buttons to include your current sales tax rate for your state. I live in New York State, mine being 8.875%. The field is located right under the price option of your Buy Now button located under Merchant Services.

1. Item name
2. Price
3. Shipping
4. Sales Tax Rate
5. Inventory
6. Profit and Loss Margin

You must type in a percentage. Ask your local sales tax office what the current rate is. You sales tax office can be found with a simple Google search 'State Sales Tax Office' (in my case adding in the search 'NYS').

A PayPal Merchant Account includes a Virtual Terminal for accepting Credit Card Payments over the phone. Not everyone is qualified for this service. Remember your are bonded as a sales agent to handle credit card numbers. Only charge customers cards when you have permission. Do not charge your clients when you are using saved card numbers you were not supposed to keep record of. This all goes on your merchant credit and you can lose your right to handle card numbers.

Invoices. When you have your customer emails all in one place get used to sending out a PayPal invoice to your prospected clients. A simple invoice saying 'Computer Break Fix' Amount: $60 and you can require payments up front. If you have a client that you need to break fix once per week ask them to complete a subscription link. Subscription links bill either once per week or once per month and read like the following. 'Pre-Paid Break Fix Services' Amount $60 Billed: Weekly This saves your client a lot of time and many of them do not want to write checks.

Buy Now buttons. Making a web site with your services, a detailed description and a Buy Now button located at the bottom of your ad is recommended. Most clients will not pay until they speak with you over the phone and make an appointment but Buy Now buttons add an extra level to having new clients.

Do not's:

1. Do not use donation buttons. These are for non-for-profit foundations such as schools and charities. PayPal will require to see documentation that you are a non-for-profit organization and you could lose your PayPal account. Keep your invoices accurate.
2. Do not send invoices for services not requested. Do not charge credit cards to anything except for your credit card machine.
3. Never charge a client's card to your personal cell phone bill regardless of what the circumstances may be, even if you are in jeopardy of losing your phone. PayPal debit card is perfect for this. Charge your client through PayPal and pay your bills debit.

Chapter 11: Start an E-Commerce Web Site.

While you may have a great web site with **OfficeLive.com** with your shared office space, online documents and contacts book all in one place you need an e-commerce store front. For this there is no better way to go than Yahoo Stores. Of course **GoDaddy.com** is the competition and of course if you are an eBay man than nothing beats eBay Pro Stores, but for the down to earth sales professional on a schedule, I recommend Yahoo e-commerce stores with their state of the art inventory management API express checkout for your clients and for businesses with a bigger budget search engine marketing, I recommend Yahoo!!

1. Go to **Stores.Yahoo.com**
2. Check out the different pricing options. $9.95 Domain, Business email is extra. Just go ahead and order a Business web site with email and shopping cart for $34.95 per month billed to your card.

You will get a Store Manager and an Item Manager. For former eBay users, a Yahoo Store is a dream. You can add an unlimited quantity of items to your store without paying extra on your bill every month. Your Yahoo!! Store can be jam packed with items, make your own categories.

Tip: For a large variety of store layout options give yahoo a call and ask for different templates for Layout. The standard store template is the first one available. Yahoo has been hosting e-commerce stores for over ten years now. They have tech support agents available 24 hours per day.

Now onto step two, customizing our e-commerce store for our computer repair clients.

As we looked at earlier our store must have items to choose from. Fans, I am a little older now and I customized my store for telephone lessons and in person consultations as we saw earlier in this book…

Telephone Computer Lessons $20

Coffee House Consultation $35

Telephone and Internet Chess Lessons $20

But we can do the same thing with A+ Computer Repair by following these guidelines:

1. Make a package deal for your clients such as on site service repair $60 per site visit.
2. Upgrades $90
3. Diagnostics $65
4. Hardware swap $75 plus parts
5. Anti-virus install and configuration $69

It is worth while to get savy with excel sheets, Microsoft Office as well as making PDF documents and scanning. We all start out as computer repair men but while working in offices, I was always asked to help scan and make PDF doc's books, bulletins, brochures, posters. As the years passed by, I started spending all of my time on the desktop publishing aspects of running an office. I just label all of my office services under one category…

Microsoft Office Specialist $20 per hour. I let my clients figure out what services to order.

A good example of computer repair package deals are as follows:

1. 1 XP workstation $60
2. 10 XP workstations $600
3. XP workstations plus server repair and configuration $1,200
4. Server to Server Virtualization Please Inquire
5. Server Failed Server Busy Please Inquire
6. Email Server Configuration Please Inquire
7. Office Computer Backup 1 workstation $60
8. Office Computer Backup 10 workstations $600
9. Office System Upgrade Patch Anti-Virus and Ghost 1 workstation $69
10. Office System Upgrade Patch Anti-Virus and Ghost 10 workstation $699
11. Router Configuration Wireless 1 router $60
12. Printer Install and Configuration $60
13. Printer Cleaning, Maintenance and Repair $60 per printer

These rates vary because there is such a wide variety of arrangements your clients can have at the office. State your rates clearly. I state mine at $20 per hour for in office computer repair. You are a contractor by definition so expect almost 100% of the time your client is going to bargain the prices.

Another approach is the prepaid pricing option. This is much easier to organize and put into your shopping cart.

1. Minimum 3 hours $60
2. 10 hours Pre-Paid $200
3. 40 hours Pre-Paid $800

Most corporate clients will just pay the $800 and ask you to keep a time sheet of how many hours you worked so far. A small home office will pay for one, or at the most ten hours Pre-Paid but not much else. Getting your services around your local business district is very recommended. You can only charge so much for a home user. A friend of mine from graduate school got a job working for a firm in lower Manhattan and now gets a salary of $195,000 per year. He no longer needs to freelance with his Yahoo!! Store.

Chapter 12: Have a Tax ID? Get a Business Phone & Email.

Unlike a personal cell phone, using your social, once you get a Tax ID you can apply for a business phone. The business phone application look like the following…

1. Your name
2. Business name
3. Tax ID **-*******
4. Address
5. Current phone number

The phone carrier for many years now cannot require a social. While there is a credit check to see how many phones you qualify for, it is easy enough to pass; as long as you have a current phone contract, you should be good to go.

I got my business phone from Sprint, but will eventually switch over to Verizon. The Verizon company owns many land lines where I live in NYC and I am not playing favorites and am simply trying to run a successful computer business, so going with the land line company is the only way to go. You can inquire at the local phone company in the town where you live to find out which company owns the land lines, and which company is right for you.

Just like any new phone be ready to pay your setup fees and have all the money up front. You don't want to be like one of those guys from around the neighborhood that has a charged off phone because he could not pay the fee and is always broke. Set your cash aside and order your business phone when you are ready.

Business email is much easier to order. You cannot legally vend out of a personal email, so do not forget to order a business email. Most of them are relatively affordable and cost between $29.95 per year up to roughly $100 for a year. It also depends on how many mail boxes you are ordering.

Chapter 13: Make a local flyer campaign.

This is where advertising gets more fun. You can go out and meet people, get your company name out there and make some money.

A flyer consists of the following elements, a logo, a title, a company name, your phone number, a short description and a lot of graphics.

Shop USA Network

Web Site Design & IT Services

347-451-1154

Image of a computer goes here

Short description about your company. Get your web site designed by a Microsoft Office Specialist. Our team has many years proven success fixing computers and designing web sites. Order a web site for only $200 down. Computer fix minimum $40 per house call.

We accept PayPal, just ask.

I live in a major city, so our town requires flyering permits. Your town most likely does not. As long as you have a Tax ID you are legal to flyer. In NYC if you are caught flyering without a permit, and get a summons, bringing proof of your Tax ID to court should beat your case in most cases. This is the city's cruel way of collecting their taxes.

Flyering on private property is with permission of the owner of the land has nothing to do with City Permits or Permissions at all. If you want to hang your flyer at the local Laundromat this is with permission of owner/ manager. The same goes for the local University or Coffee shop. With permission of owner.

My chess club is located on a private property. I often get asked the question about how often our permits are checked, or how often the local cop comes around to see who is hanging. The answer is never. Our chess club is on private property. This is one of the laws that makes America free of an imperialist army sweeping through and taking away our privileges. We do not have to ask for city permission to flyer or play chess on a private property.

I recommend staying away from street poles all together. Although you may see the ad for the local moving company on street poles this is tricky business. The street poles are owned by the city and it is a dangerous business to tag them without permission. Get caught doing that who knows, they may tow your car.

Organize as event at a local place or even a barbeque at your mother's house and give everyone a flyer for your services. Go to your friend's show at the local pub and give out your flyer as well.

Musicians are well known for doing this, but make a separate MySpace account for your business. You may see all the time,
MySpace.com/MusicianNameHere
FaceBook.com/MusicianNameHere
Make a MySpace and FaceBook account for your business and then send out a link to everyone you know. Once you have organized a MySpace event bring a print out of 100 or more of your flyers and bring them along for the show.

For help with proof reading your flyer see **Chapter 3:** Hiring a writer.

Chapter 14: More on Web Sites.

To make your job easier break your web sites down into a few of these categories.

1. Product pages with small icons and a price list
2. Product pages with more information provided
3. Pages with '**Buy Now**' buttons and a phone number
4. A Shop

Now we have a bunch of product pages. Now we will write our company main page and services page and include tons of links to our products and services.

Home Page of your computer repair company

Link to **Product Page** with pricing options as discussed earlier

More Info page, a detailed description of your product

About Us page

Links to more products

About Us page

Link to **Contact Page**

Link to **Shop**

Now we have a whole set of Product Pages but we do not have a shop. A shop is a place where you keep all of the links to your items in one neat place for the reader to be able to browse through the pages without any trouble. You want every single item for sale on your web site located in your Shop. You also want to write a product page for every single item in your shop. This may be very time consuming but this is something that your clients are expecting to see.

Here is an example as previously quoted in the best seller, 'Sam Sloan Teaches Web Site Design'.

Insert a table object, and insert an image within the table object. Center the objects in your table.

Give the table a border and add in the text for the price, a **'Buy Now'** button and a **'More Info'** button. The **'Buy Now'** button links to a PayPal page and the **'More Info'** button links to your product page and more information is provided.

Your shop gets an extension. Either a prefix or a suffix to your domain.

A prefix looks like this,

http://shop.yourstorename.com

My shop uses a suffix as an extension.

http://ShopUSANetwork.com/shop.aspx

The aspx extension is a product of Microsoft which makes my job updating my web site very easy. You can get yourself a Microsoft powered web site by going to www.OfficeLive.com and you can add in a domain name, preferably your company name for $14.95 per year.

The template includes really neat modules for updating your site and also has a shared work space for inviting clients to come and look at your stored documents.

So we made our web site and one customer complained that the description was deceiving. There are a few simple rules of thumb to follow. Make your price tags very easy to read. Put your descriptions right below the item for sale, or even easier, get a Yahoo store and the template will require that you paste your description right into one neat place. The down side to the system is your shop will have items for sale, but will be limited in how much material you can provide to your readers. Solution? Get one Office Live site for your customers to read more about your service, and one Yahoo store for processing payments. These are your clients remember. They may be on the phone with you for very many hours, so you do not want to scare away a client by making it too difficult for them to order, but on the other hand not enough information to provided.

All of this information must be provided in writing because we are a refund driven people. Everyone that goes to a shop these days looks at a way to find a mistake in the text and get a refund. You want to be as clear as possible in what your services are as not to confuse anyone.

Your contact us page should also be really easy to read and have a simple email link. I recommend staying away from forms is the recommendation of many Office Live representatives I have spoken with. When you create a form your information basically goes into an in between point between your web site and your email account and lingers there until it is sent. Programmers have tried their best to have forms be able to catch all of the information but never seem to work correctly.

Contact information should go as follows.

Company Name

Contact Name

Business Phone

Business Address

Email Link

I would throw in a credit card order form while you are at it. Include an address where clients can mail in their card number. It is a really nice day when you wake up and find a surprise order form in your mail box when you were otherwise going to stay home for the day and have some quiet time reading, just a pinch short on gas money.

Chapter 15: Open a Business Banking Account.

I don't know where you live, but in my city Capital One and Chase are going around opening everyone Business Banking and eCommerce web sites with merchant accounts. Open yourself a Business Banking account ASAP as many clients are going to write checks to your company name. You can side step this by providing your first and last name but you will not be paid as much. You may even have to turn down corporate clients. Opening a business bank account and open up for business. While you can only charge your client $60 per call as an individual, as a corporation your client can pay you in the upwards of thousands because they get a nice tax write off for their expenses.

You can get an eCommerce web site through Chase, or other services such as Quick Books.

You can stay with your PayPal account or order yourself a Merchant account through your bank. Remember there is a contract included, so stick with PayPal until you have a demand from your clients for more volume that requires you keep your merchant account at your bank.

Chapter 16: Don't Forget Self Employment Tax 27%.

I live in New York State where self employment tax is 27%. This rate varies state by state. Ask you tax man for the exact amount.

Be wary to withhold your self employment tax. Every penny of this money is collectable by the IRS. Failure to report your self employment tax could lead to your business being frozen.

For corporate clients, ask that they give you a 1099-MISC at the end of the year. This makes your job easier in filing your taxes. I am strict enough about this I plain old will not accept a client that does not have the ability to write a 1099-MISC. I simply provide my SS card and my photo ID to the payroll secretary when it is time to send employees and contractors their earnings statements.

Tips on Taxes: Overpay your tax. It has been twice now I was a little behind on my taxes but because I was making an overpayment. Never write any extra deductions like phone bills or office bills. Most of these things are not deductable in the first place and you wind up owing more money later. One other way to overpay your tax is not to claim federal withholdings. Even though the company you worked for most likely withheld 10% of your pay you are better off not claiming your withholdings. This is money in the bank. Not a single American business ever got into trouble while the IRS actually owed them money. This is all referred to as over payment. A freelance contractor that overpays his tax can never be pushed out of business in any state.

Chapter 17: Congratulations, You Are Self Employed.

We have the following after reading this book that make us self employed:

1. A business name
2. A Tax ID
3. A web site and business card
4. A business phone and email
5. A PayPal business account
6. Business Banking
7. A classified ad
8. Declared our business on our taxes via Turbo Tax

Now that we have all of the following we are officially self employed. Throw yourself a little party and invite some friends over because you no longer have a boss. Don't turn the music up too loud because even though we own a business does not mean we own a house. Don't want to get evicted.

Work for one entire year as a computer repair man, fixing computers all over the place, charging cash, credit cards, you name it. Get your flyers and links to your web site all over town. When the year is done and you file your taxes on Turbo Tax including your income from your business you are officially self employed.

Chapter 18: A few tips on things to watch out for. Scam Alerts, Fraud.

Online fraud and credit card fraud are a lot less likely to be a victim of today then we were even three years ago. Back in 2006 I put a painting for sale on eBay of an original artwork of an American solider in Iraq hugging a baby. Someone bought the painting for two credit card payments of $700 each. I shipped the paintings and went back about my usual business. One week later I got the following email,

Notice of Chargeback:** Your account is -$1,400

Boy was I surprised. I did not think it was possible to refund the payments. I contacted PayPal and they said the person had reversed the charges using his card company. I asked if his account could be held accountable for the damage and the answer was no. He was just a random person from California with very little identifying information on his PayPal account. I had to pay back the money out of my own pocket. PayPal is very nice to work with and allowed me plenty of time to pay the balance. When I was done, they mailed me a PayPal business debit card as a nice thank you.

That was 2006, this is today, zero refunds except for specific items purchased mail order through eBay. See the letter on the next page.

Hello Shop USA Network.LLC,

We have concluded our investigation of the Buyer Complaint for the
transaction detailed below.

According to the User Agreement, PayPal's Buyer Complaint **Policy applies only to the shipment of goods and not to services and other intangible goods**. For that reason, we are unable to take any action regarding this complaint. We encourage you to work directly with the buyer to resolve this issue.

Transaction Details
Buyer's name: ####-#########-#####
Buyer's email: ######-##############
Transaction ID: 6PS9241285487730N

Transaction date: Mar 27, 2011
Transaction amount: $50.00 USD
Your transaction ID: 6DF666608H809653W
Case number: PP-001-273-057-963

Refund amount: $0.00 USD

Victory!!! The charge back scam artists can no longer get their money refunded. I just finished reading a newspaper report about Kmart complaining about over $1 Million of charge backs per year after the customer left the store. The thief can no longer use PayPal resolution for these means.

2628851R00045

Printed in Great Britain
by Amazon.co.uk, Ltd.,
Marston Gate.